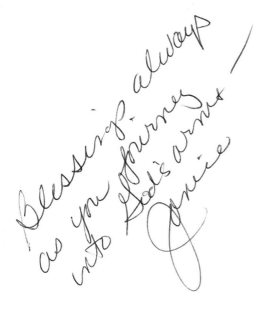

Blessings always
as you journey
into God's arms

Janice

D0114650

BESTSELLER

AFFAIRS of the HEART

God's Messages to the World

J. I. Willett

Affairs of the Heart – God's Messages to the World
Copyright © 2013 by J. I. Willett

Published by J.I. Willett

Cover design by Pam Brown-Villaruz

Book design by Aspen Svec - www.1260productions.com

ISBN: 978-0615-86974-2-51695

Printed in the USA

ACKNOWLEDGEMENTS

My deepest appreciation to Father Brendan Williams who was instrumental in bringing me back to the Catholic religion, introducing me to charismatic healing, and becoming a friend and inspiration for me to follow God on the journey to write this book. Father Williams not only opened his heart to me, but also to many of my family members and close friends during their times of need. He is truly a blessing and a gift to us all.

I extend my thanks and love to my wonderful family and my great friends for their continuous support, understanding, encouragement, and uplifting testimonials.

My gratitude to the very creative Pam Brown-Villaruz, who was divinely placed in my path to design the beautiful cover of this book.

A special thank you to Laura Carlson, who diligently worked on the final review, suggestions and improvements to this book; and to Aspen Svec who through layout and typesetting made this book come alive.

Many thanks to Rocco for his guidance; as well as to those who ever so briefly crossed my path, unknowingly messengers of God delivering answers to my prayers.

Contents

Private Revelations 7

Preface 11

Introduction 21

My First Revelation 37

My Second Revelation 47

From Darkness to Light 53

Guidelines from God 63

Everything Has to Do With Numbers 73

Intercessor 83

Healing Mass 91

The Ten Commitments 103

Why Me Lord? 113

Divine Intervention 121

In Conclusion 139

Closing 145

PRIVATE REVELATIONS

*F*rom early childhood our family elders have taught us that religion is a set of practices or rituals. Although their true meaning may not be understood at that young age, we begin to form the belief that there is one creator or higher power.

Some different names that have been used around the world through the ages for this Higher Power are Abba, Yahweh, Elohim, Lord, and God.

In much of Christianity, the belief is in the Holy Trinity … God in three "persons": God whom we cannot see; Jesus, the Son of God, who took human form; and the Holy Spirit who speaks to our hearts.

Despite our numerous titles, we do agree on the oneness of a single maker, and all we can do is to give Him glory.

The purpose of the following pages is to share my private revelations to inspire and encourage you to turn more wholeheartedly to God and the lordship of Christ in your life; as well as embrace more intensely the divine revelation contained in the Scriptures to correctly guide us on our faith journey to the Promised Land of Heaven.

PREFACE

*I*n the fall of 2007 I felt such a low in my life … my marriage was failing, I was no longer enjoying my job, and I felt lost about the direction for my future. My soul was troubled; I was floundering. It seemed I couldn't go another day feeling this emptiness. There were so many questions about my purpose here on earth that I couldn't answer. I needed to find myself. I needed to search for a deeper, richer meaning to my life because up till that time I was totally unfulfilled. I knew that God had made me a giving person and I wanted to give, but the more I gave, the more people took and took and took from me… until my soul was drained. I knew this couldn't go on anymore and I prayed for direction.

Because I had a history with God providing answers to me when I prayed for them, I decided to go to my church to sit in silence and hopefully gain some insight. To my surprise, what I got was far beyond what I ever anticipated or was asking for.

With the peacefulness and comfort that St. Veronica Church afforded me, I stood before the wooden carved statue of Jesus who seemed to look upon me with welcoming eyes. All the candles on both sides of the statue were lit, emitting a warming red glow, and the rays of the sun through the stained glass windows bathed the darkened church with multifaceted colors of soft light.

I looked up to Jesus and began crying as I spoke my concerns in silence. As with all of my communications since childhood, I did not use my voice, I expressed my thoughts in my mind. I waited quietly to hear God's response.

I can best analogize this process of divine communication to recounting a movie to others: we first hear the words and see the images in our mind when organizing the story.

When God spoke to me in the confines of my mind, He urged me to start bringing a pad on which to take notes because this would be a lengthy process. I rarely questioned Him in the past, but on that day I needed to ask Him why. He concisely informed me that I was to write down his messages and inspirations to share with the world. He said I was His intercessor—one whom, through prayer, intervenes for another.

He further explained that the transcriptions would be made into the book He had, years prior, told me I would be writing, and which He'd entitled *Affairs of the Heart*.

I must confess that when He previously informed me of the title, I thought the book was going to be about human love stories. Little did I know it would be on divine passion, God's intense love for us and His desire to prevent us from destruction. It was to be a book about ourselves, our families, our communities, our countries, and our world as we know it.

I was overwhelmed and frightened. This was a huge responsibility put on me and I wasn't sure He chose the right person. The situation felt surreal. The Lord was challenging me to step outside the box, out of my comfort zone, which required me to set aside my fear of failure and ridicule by nonbelievers and do exactly as I was instructed.

I remember crying and looking up to the ceiling saying, "Why me Lord? I am with faults, imperfect, not worthy to be chosen for such an important task."

He responded, "You are to be a guide, which will allow others to find their way."

Who am I to say no?

And so I began my love affair with the Lord. From that day forward, I went to church nearly every day for approximately three months, receiving God's messages at St. Veronica Church.

Day after day, week after week, month after month, my love for Him grew deeper and deeper. I would awake every morning with such excitement, looking forward to my time with Him. Some days I would run so fast to stand before the Statue of Jesus, that God's voice would boom in my ears. *"Slow down, Janice! Just stop, pause, and slow down!"* I could hear the love in His voice, as a child might hear a parent caringly speak a command. I could tell He was pleased with my enthusiasm, yet He knew I needed to learn how to slow down at times and just pause.

Our visits varied in time from half an hour to hours. In high school I learned how to write shorthand, and it came in quite handy because at times He would speak so quickly that I would ask Him to slow down. He would just laugh and tell me I could keep up and keep writing. There were also times when I would think we were done, close my journal, and start to leave when

I'd hear the smile in His voice as He would say (and quite often I might add), "Janice, we're not done yet."

When we were done with each daily session, I couldn't wait to get home to transcribe all my notes onto my computer. I had started to share some of the daily messages with a few people, and gradually I had a small group of family and friends looking forward to receiving His daily word via email. Their testimonials were inspirations that encouraged me to stay on the path God chose for me.

My many journals from the daily sessions took me on a journey ... an unexpected pilgrimage. I embraced becoming closer to Him. I soon realized He wasn't just my best friend, He was my mentor, my Savior, and the love of my life. For the first time ever, a moment of clarity came over me: I had always loved God; however, I had never been *in love* with God, truly loved Him more than anything on this earth.

I am blessed to be a part of the Word of the Lord, and thankful that He trusts me to deliberately and honestly transcribe His Word. It is an honor to be His chosen vessel to pass these messages on to you.

God is the most glorious, loving, wonderful, humorous, concerned overseer of His people, His community of worshippers.

These messages are universal, all-inclusive, and all-embracing. They are for all mankind to share. It is never too late to open your hearts to love, compassion and unity.

Let His words lead us and educate us. In its most simplistic form these words represent the Grace He sheds upon us. It is that same Grace that He lovingly asks us to share with one another.

Please read, absorb, follow, instill, and spread His glorious statements throughout mankind, for without God we are nothing.

He asks us to listen. He keeps saying to me "Now is the time," and I hear the urgency in His voice.

Since receiving and transcribing His Word for this book, I have found more peace than ever before, and more moments of clarity. I am the calmest I have ever been, and I look forward to each day's new surprises, miracles and messages. But most of all, I look forward to world peace.

This has been an inspiring time of growth for me, and I hope you will feel the same after reading this book.

As God said to me, "Expect the unexpected. Now is the time. Be prepared."

Are you?

INTRODUCTION

*M*y parents met during the mid 1940s in New York City at Dale's Dance Studio, which was located on Broadway near 35th Street. It was a second floor walk up divided into a small waiting area and several small private instruction rooms.

My mother, a natural beauty with a fashion model's figure, was quite talented at dancing. With her smooth and precise moves, she quickly became one of Dale Dance Studio's key instructors, teaching all the popular dances at that time such as the Foxtrot, the Tango, the Waltz, and the Charleston.

My dad, a handsome Italian from Brooklyn who had no idea how to dance, had been asked by his zany cousin, Ben, to take the dance classes with him. As much as my father tried to resist his cousin's efforts, Ben finally coerced him into going. My father was also quite hesitant to make plans with Ben, because the last time his cousin twisted his arm, my father ended up in restaurant in Chinatown at 1:00 a.m. trying to order a hamburger when moo shu pork was the closest thing to meat on the menu! Dad could only imagine what the dance studio visit would turn into since it was always some type of adventure with Ben.

After the breathless ascent to the second floor, my father and Ben entered the humid dance studio's reception area that boasted well-used wooden floors. After registering for their class, they were given numbers. They then waited their turn by sitting on small, uncomfortable wooden chairs, bringing back memories of grammar school. With droplets of perspiration forming on their heads—despite the open windows—an eclectic mix of music emanated from the various studios creating a sense of audio confusion.

When my father's number was called, he accompanied the next available instructor to her individual classroom, which had small observation cutouts in the doors. My father asked his instructor what the small cutouts were for, and she jokingly responded, "It's so that the boss is sure that we're dancing."

Ben, who was always looking for a new adventure, quit after the first lesson, stating that these dances weren't as exciting as he had thought they would be. My dad would have quit as well, but he was so smitten with his stunning instructor that he knew he had to continue the weekly classes to get to know her better. That instructor, of course, was my mother.

During that time my mom was commuting an hour by train to and from her home in the central New Jersey town of Carteret. Once she mentioned this to my father, he made sure to sign up for the last dance of the evening in order to have the opportunity to walk her to the train station ... "After all, it just wasn't safe for such an attractive woman to be walking alone in the city after dark."

These after class walks turned into mini dates, and soon my mother and father were spending time together grabbing coffee at a little nearby diner, where they became regulars. Rusty, the counter server, took such a liking to these lovebirds that he began slipping them a slice of pie and two forks at no extra charge.

Over time, the dating became more serious, and my father was continuously driving back and forth an hour each way to visit with my mother. After several months, they realized they deeply loved each other and decided to marry, live in Carteret, and start a family. As the topic of religion had never been discussed, they were in for quite a surprise.

My mother, a practicing Presbyterian, and my father, a non-practicing Catholic, were informed by his devout Catholic parents that there would be no marriage unless my mother converted to Catholicism and promised that their children would be baptized in the Catholic Church.

And so my folks got married, and so my sister and I were baptized Catholic.

When I was just two years old, my family moved from my mother's hometown of Carteret to a little fixer-upper bungalow on a back road in a rural area of southern New Jersey.

About a mile up the road was a two story historical Presbyterian Church perched on a steep hill, surrounded by a large cemetery, mature trees, and wrought iron fencing. Due to the vast acreage, there were two gated entrances, one from our road and one from the intersecting road.

Being that my father had no interest in pursuing Catholicism, and my mother really had no understanding of Catholic rituals, she decided to join the Presbyterian Church on the hill. Because my mother enjoyed attending regular services, she decided to enroll my sister and me in the Bible school and Sunday school programs. My sister and I attended Sunday school until our early teens, at which time we each received our Holy Confirmations.

All during my early Sunday school years I was so inspired by the stories of Jesus and God that it made me want to pursue a deeper relationship with them. One of the things I loved was praising God through hymns, especially taking delight in singing "Jesus Loves Me." I somehow knew He was and always would be my best friend.

At the age of six or seven, I had an overwhelming spiritual experience while riding my bicycle home on our desolate country road. The day was balmy and there wasn't a cloud in the sky. As I was approaching a heavily wooded area between the open farm fields harbored by deep drainage ditches, I heard a woman's voice gently calling to me from above and to my right.

When I looked in that direction, I saw the most beautiful angel dressed in white hovering over the woodlands, seemingly bigger than the trees themselves. The base of her flowing garment faded from the sky into the treetops. She was absolutely radiant against the blue sky, smiling down at me holding an open book that reminded me of a hymnal. Staring at her in reverence,

I heard an orchestration of beautiful church music, exceedingly to the type I heard many years later coming from the large pipe organ in St. Patrick's Cathedral... and it was awesome.

I had goose bumps all over my body, and I could hardly see through the tears welling in my eyes as I flew home on my bike. The pedals couldn't move fast enough to match the excitement of this amazing experience. I couldn't wait to tell my mother!

When I approached the garage, my feet kept their momentum as I dropped my bike and ran through the house yelling with enthusiasm all the way to the kitchen where my mother was preparing dinner. Gasping for air between my words, I relayed the wonders I had just experienced. My mother was so happy for me, smiling and listening intently, absorbing every little detail.

Because of my spiritual appreciation growing up, I chose to return to the Sunday school as a teacher for three years, until a new regime of church elders took over. By this time I was grown with children of my own, and I found it rewarding to teach the preschoolers about God and Jesus. Their innocence and unwavering love confirmed and strengthened my faith.

The new church elders required their teachers to attend the main church services following Sunday school, which would force my children to be in day care on Sunday as well as during the week. And so I left the Presbyterian Church.

I didn't go back to church for many years, although I continued my relationship with the Lord through scripture and prayer. I didn't find a place of worship I was comfortable with until moving to the neighboring town of Howell, New Jersey ... and that church was St. Veronica's.

The unobtrusive church, built in 1963, was set far off the road; and the rectory was mostly hidden from the highway by overgrown tree branches. The sign for the church at that time was so small and obscure that if it weren't for the magnetic pull I felt each time I drove past the property, I probably would never have been aware of its presence.

Week after week, month after month, I drove past this church, resisting its strong pull, ignoring its invitation to share in what was yet unknown to me. I resisted because I was baptized Catholic, but had no knowledge of the Church's rituals. I feared appearing foolish until one day in June of 1998 when I was in tremendous abdominal pain.

During one of my extreme pain episodes, I had to actually stop driving until the pain subsided. I happened to look to my right and saw St. Veronica's, so I decided to rest in the church and pray for my healing. When I entered this sanctuary through one of its multiple doors, I was stunned by the beauty and peacefulness I encountered. I surveyed the vast vaulted ceiling and then the crucifix above the altar. As I took all of this in, I slowly turned my gaze behind me and saw a carved, illuminated statue of Jesus, inviting me to Him.

I slowly shuffled toward Him, dropping to my knees, tears quickly flooding my eyes as I asked Him to help me. Suddenly a sense of peace came over me and I knew that I would be healed soon … although I had no idea how.

When I returned home I found myself prompted to search the Internet's medical websites for information regarding my pain … whereupon I reached a doctor who surgically corrected my misdiagnosed problem within days.

While convalescing at home after the extensive surgical procedure, the pain became unbearable and the medications were of no help. I decided to call the priest of St. Veronica Church and ask him to pray with me for healing—after the extraordinary response to my prayers with Jesus only days before, how could I go wrong?

When I called the rectory I spoke to Father Williams who asked me what my needs were, and I replied, "Father, I know that God comes not too soon nor too late for a purpose and that many have endured suffering greater than mine;

however, I am in so much pain right now I'd rather be dead."

Acknowledging my statement with his calming voice, Father Williams asked how soon I could meet at his office, located in the rectory. It was late evening and I physically couldn't drive, so I told the priest I would have my sister take me in the morning. Never did I realize that this chance meeting would be the next part of my journey toward writing this book.

My sister slowly and carefully guided me into her vehicle at 8:30 a.m. for the thankfully short ride to the rectory. We parked in front of the tan brick building and gingerly made our way up the steps and into the small foyer. The short priest, who spoke with an Irish brogue, welcomed us with open arms and a smile that emanated the presence of God's love and reassured me I would be healed both physically and spiritually.

Through his divine gifts, Father Williams made that day the first day of the rest of my life as we three arranged our wooden chairs in a close circle to hold hands and pray. Anointing my forehead with Holy Oil, he chanted barely audible words that seemed to speak to my spirit. I felt intense warmth radiating from inside my body – suddenly feeling as though I was floating in the clouds, pain-free. I was vaguely aware of the tears flowing down my face from the overwhelming joy of this experience, and I didn't want to open my eyes for fear of losing the moment. When I did, I saw my sister's face and she, too, was crying. Something powerful was happening in our circle that was nearly impossible to describe. Father Williams, my sister, and I stood in embrace, giving thanks to God for His intervention through our prayers.

Father Williams led my sister and me from his office, suggesting we visit the adjoining adoration chapel where we could sit peacefully and contemplate our experience before we headed out into the noisy, busy world.

Through these prayers I gained a new found strength physically and spiritually, although I must say I was still a bit overwhelmed by such a huge experience. With God's intense healing powers, I was soon back on my feet, and I decided to join St. Veronica Church, attending weekend services and monthly healing masses on a regular basis.

After approximately one year of attending a church where I felt I belonged, I knew it was time to prepare to receive my First Holy Communion. I attended RCIA classes (The Rite of Christian Initiation of Adults) at St. Veronica Church.

As part of our initiation, two nights before our First Holy Communion, my classmates and I carried a very large, heavy wooden cross on our shoulders down the center aisle to the front of the church for the Good Friday Services.

The power of that experience nearly brought me to my knees, not just because the weight of the cross was nearly unbearable even with a group tending to it, but also because I was overwhelmed thinking that Jesus carried a similar cross by Himself for a much longer period of time and after being tortured. I wept. All of this immediately brought me even closer to God.

MY FIRST REVELATION

*I*n June of 2008, while praying alone in St. Veronica Church, God revealed a symbol to me, which appeared like a snapshot in my mind.

The image contained two uneven parallel lines across the top and two vertical lines below them. A solid circle hovered above these lines, making me think it was of the sun. Because I didn't want to forget this image, I was frantically looking for something to write on. After I found a crumpled napkin in my pocket, I immediately drew the symbol. I asked God what it meant, but I received no answer. I was a little confused.

As I arrived home, I rushed to my computer to glean any information about such an image because it was so unfamiliar to me. This much I knew: it had to have a profound meaning or God would not have presented it to me.

The symbol reminded me of writing on a Chinese menu, and being that I like Chinese food, my first thought was to ask the folks at my local Chinese restaurant if they could provide a meaning to the sketched object. They didn't have a specific name for it, but they said that it wasn't a Chinese letter … it definitely was a religious symbol.

I knew I was onto something, so the Nancy Drew in me hopped into my car to drive less than a mile to a Japanese restaurant to inquire if the owners were familiar with the symbol on my napkin. They knew it was a religious church symbol—perhaps a gateway to religious secrets—but they did not know much more than that.

My curiosity now thoroughly piqued, I drove down the highway to my dry cleaners, where the Korean owners identified the mysterious figure as a religious symbol!

I was determined to solve this riddle, and realized there was a sect from Asia that I hadn't reached out to. I drove home, bolted from the car to my computer, and began looking online for the nearest Buddhist house of worship location, which—to my surprise—was only five miles from where I sat!

Back in the car I headed to the address I had found. I slowly approached the small remote plot, eyeing several monks in their traditional robes who were gardening within a chain link fence. I felt peaceful as I watched these monks float about the lawn focused on their duties. I hesitated calling to them, not wanting to disturb their serene state.

The monk closest to the road saw me and nodded in reverence for me to approach, so I met him at the fence, which was the halfway mark between the both of us. As I stood there, I asked about the symbol I had drawn. He responded in broken English that my drawing was a religious symbol pertaining to a gateway. His expression gave me a feeling that he knew I was on an important journey toward enlightenment.

I needed no more confirmations to catapult myself back in front of the computer. For hours I studied hieroglyphs and other types of symbols and then wanted to visit my local library to gather more information.

I then concluded my investigation through the stack of library books when I confirmed the drawing was that of the Torii, a Japanese symbol from the Shinto religion, representing the gateway between the physical and spiritual worlds.

The Shinto believe the Torii represents the gate to all mysteries. The Gate is made in three parts, consisting of two upright supports and a double-barred cross member (a lintel) … combined representing deity known as Kami, which means *divine being* to the Shinto.

Figure 1. The floating Torii, located in Miyajima, Japan.

I find it rather impressive that twice in Japan's recent history the country was devastated with massive destruction, yet the Torii stood solid as a representation of God *(Nagasaki, Japan, 1945 and Otsuchi, Japan, 2011).*

Appearing most similar to the Torii gate is Tian (天), one of the oldest Chinese terms which means *sky, heaven, God,* and *celestial.* This character is used in Japanese, Chinese, and Korean languages as a logogram, a symbol that represents a word or an object. This may be part of why the people of the different Asian cultures I questioned knew its general meaning.

43

The Tian symbol made popular during the Han Dynasty represents or translates as path or way in Taoism (modernly known as Daoism), which focuses on the relationship between humanity and the cosmos.

The gate is also a metaphor for the humanities, the study of who we were, who we are, and who we hope to become. Thus the humanities are a gateway to our past and to our future.

Obviously the Korean, Japanese, and Chinese people I spoke with didn't know the symbol's specific meaning, but they did know that my sketch was of an important religious nature.

I wondered why God would show a person of Catholic faith and European descent an Asian symbol. I believe it was to show me that all religions that believe in God or a higher being face mysteries of their faith. I now realized how this tied in with my own religious beliefs. Catholicism celebrates the mysteries of faith, and coincidentally, the word catholic is derived from the Greek word, Katholikos, originally meaning universal.

I felt that God was using my voice to speak to the world, and the Torii demonstrated that despite all the current and future world devastation, we need to keep our focus on God, whatever we may call him.

Could the Torii gate be God's representation of the gates of heaven, the passage from one world to another? Could it represent the unity of our various religions under one God, uniting the world of Eastern and Western religions?

Perhaps.

MY SECOND REVELATION

Several months after the Torii gate research was completed, I was shown another vision while in a prayerful state. It was a universal symbol for mankind: a circle representing the head, double horizontal outstretched arms and two vertical lines representing a pair of legs. It resembled the Torii symbol!

I immediately realized the upward arms represented a person reaching up as if to glorify God, and I heard His commanding voice say to me, "Lift your arms. Lift them up to Me, your God. Lift them up high and rejoice in eternal life."

Several days later as I again stood before the blessed statue of Jesus, I was given yet another vision, this one of a cross composed of red roses—three down and one on each side— along with a single green-leaved vine that wrapped across it.

49

This seemed important, so I sketched it on my pad. God indicated the drawing was to become the cover for His book, and so I hurried out of the church, back to my house, and sat at my desk so I could prepare a color rendering. When I was done, the beauty of this rendering caused me to lean back in awe, nearly taking my breath away!

I was so excited with my new finding that I was compelled to do more research on the Internet to find the meaning of the roses and vine. The vine symbolized Jesus as the source of life to the world, as depicted in Christian artwork and in Bible quotes such as, *I am the vine, you are the branches (John 15:5)*. The roses represent passion and deep love, red petals associated with Jesus' blood and his crucifixion. The five red roses in the image of the cross I saw represent the five wounds Jesus bore.

Shortly after my vision of the cross, I received our first Sunday of Lent church bulletin. You can only imagine the chills I got.

Figure 2. St. Veronica's church bulletin, received shortly after my vision of the cross.

(Photo courtesy of John Patrick Publishing.)

FROM DARKNESS TO LIGHT

*T*he low point in my life that I referred to earlier, which began this personal journey, was marked by unexplainable fear and doubt. I realized that God had been calling me to Him, like a parent to their child, to bring me from the darkness to the light of His grace.

In the empty church bathed with the colorful afternoon light, I had my pad and pen in hand to await His next message, and thanked God in prayer for this opportunity.

He responded, "No, thank you! Thank you for always keeping me in your heart from when you were little. Through all your hardships you always loved Me and believed I was there."

I continued, "Lord, I find the process of letting go so difficult … of things, emotions … in order to move forward on my spiritual journey."

He said, "When you're willing to give it up, you'll get it all back."

I was a bit perplexed by this statement until my dream that evening …

I was in a jewelry store on a dark deserted street in the center of town. I didn't know why I was there, but I was standing by the large glass window at the front of the store, when a group of thieves rushed through the adjoining door wielding guns, ordering me and the other people nearby to give up our valuables. I wanted to hide the expensive ring on my finger before they noticed, but I realized by not giving it up I might die.

I desperately tried to think of what to do as I focused my gaze out the window where I stood. There, in front of my eyes, was an empty truck parked across the street. Quickly, I thrust the ring at one of the robbers as I bolted out the door and raced to the parked truck. I launched myself into the driver's seat and focused on the key in the ignition. I fired up the engine and accelerated through the thick of night.

After I traversed the dense blackness for what seemed like an eternity, the darkness lifted like fog on a lake and the scenery slowly became visible.

I turned my attention to the discomfort in my outer left thigh, just inside where my jean's pocket lay. I could feel an object when I ran my hand over the area, so I reached into my pocket and removed what seemed to be the same ring I had given up to the robbers! At that moment I heard a strong, but gentle, voice fill the truck. "When you're willing to give it up, you'll get it all back."

Upon waking I grabbed my journal and began penning this dream. It was then I realized I had been in the "dark" so to speak, a dark night of the soul. I had been materialistically robbed of my peace of mind. By giving up my attachment to the physical world, I could be saved like in my dream, where I risked operating a truck I didn't know how to drive through blackness where I couldn't see, travelling to a destination unknown. Call it blind faith or trust, but I moved forward and eventually there was light, yet I still had no knowledge of where the road would take me.

As I recalled moving away from the darkness into the light, I thought of how, *the Lord giveth and the Lord taketh away (Job 1:21)*. What I once put value in, when I finally gave it up, He provided back for me. In the beginning of the dream, the ring, to me, symbolized material possessions, but by the end of my dream, the ring symbolized a circle of love and eternal life.

I set my journal down on my nightstand and lay back to contemplate. The dream made me think of my immortality, so I asked God at what age I would die, and He responded, "You will never die."

My eyes welled with tears. I had heard the statement in all my religious teachings, but failed to truly absorb its meaning: my soul would never die!

I told God, "I have been waiting to be free, peaceful, flowing," and he quickly replied, "Yes, you withstood the thorns of the heart and now is your time to shine." I not only heard, but also felt the love that surrounded me and warmed my soul.

Another dream that moved me from darkness to light showed me that I needed to separate myself from certain people that were literally sucking the life out of me; those who selfishly took advantage of my kindness and gave nothing in return.

> *I was in a room lying on a stainless steel table that reminded me of the type used for autopsies or funeral preparations, cold and death-related. I was exhausted, powerless, and freezing in this large, stark,*

tiled room. Two emotionless technicians, one on each side of me, strapped each of my arms onto outstretched boards, placing me in a cruciform position—the shape of the cross. After my arms were secured, the technicians inserted intravenous needles into each of my arms with tubes running up to hanging IV bags.

I was lying there, petrified and helpless, watching as my blood was sucked out of my body, up the tubes, and into the hanging bags!

I helplessly wailed and screamed repeatedly, "I have nothing more to give. I have nothing more to give."

This dream had me shaken for days. It was God's way of saying I needed to surround myself with people who enhanced my life. In the dream, the blood represented the energy that others drained from me, and the technicians represented those individuals who were responsible for this drain.

I realized I needed to step back and assess who I surrounded myself with and who was sucking the life out of me.

I felt that God's guidance was helping me make the right choices now in my life.

GUIDELINES FROM GOD

*I*n my brokenness after my dream revelations, I prayed to God to remove my fears and give me the patience to trust Him so that He could guide me.

My prayers were answered several evenings later. As I put away the plates and glasses in my kitchen, I realized one glass was missing. I assumed it had probably gotten mixed with my good set of tumblers several weeks prior when I had a family dinner.

I walked around the corner to my mirrored dining room cupboard, and as I opened the door where the tumblers were kept, three sheets of paper glided through the air in different directions, landing haphazardly on my hardwood floor. I have to say I was pretty surprised because I don't store papers in that cabinet. And as I gathered and straightened the sheets, I became dumbstruck; the bold title on one read *Ten Guidelines From God!*

And what do you think these guidelines pertained to? Trust and patience! I don't remember ever having possession of these papers, and even if I did, I would never have placed them in my dining room cupboard!

I sat down and read the following:

Ten Guidelines From God

(author unknown)

Effective immediately, please be aware that there are changes YOU need to make in YOUR life. These changes need to be completed in order that I may fulfill My promises to you to grant you peace, joy, and happiness is this life. I apologize for any inconvenience, but after all that I am doing, this seems very little to ask of you. Please, follow these 10 guidelines.

1. QUIT WORRYING: *Life has dealt you a blow and all you do is sit and worry. Have you forgotten that I am here to take all your burdens and carry them for you? Or do you just enjoy fretting over every little thing that comes your way?*

2. PUT IT ON THE LIST: *If something needs to be done or taken care of, put it on the list. No not YOUR list. Put it on MY to-do-list. Let ME be the one to take care of the problem. I can't help you until you turn it over to Me. And although My to-do-list is long, I am after all... God. I can take care of anything you put into My hands. In fact, if the truth were ever really known, I take care of a lot of things for you that you never even realize.*

3. TRUST ME: *Once you've given your burdens to Me, quit trying to take them back. Trust in Me. Have the faith that I will take care of all your needs, your problems, and your trials. Problems with the kids? Put them on My list. Problem with finances? Put it on My list.*

Problems with your emotional roller coaster? For My sake, put it on My list. I want to help you. All you have to do is ask.

4. LEAVE IT ALONE: *Don't wake up one morning and say, "Well, I'm feeling much stronger now, I think I can handle it from here." Why do you think you are feeling stronger now? It's simple. You gave Me your burdens, and I'm taking care of them. I also renew your strength and cover you in my peace. Don't you know that if I give you these problems back, you will be right back where you started? Leave them with Me and forget about them. Just let Me do my job.*

5. TALK TO ME: *I want you to forget a lot of things. Forget what was making you crazy; forget the worry and the fretting because you know I'm in control. But there's one thing I pray you never forget: Please, don't forget to talk to Me—OFTEN! I love YOU! I want to hear your voice. I want you to include Me in on the things going on in your life. I want to hear you talk about your friends and family.*

Prayer is simply you having a conversation with Me. I want to be your dearest friend.

6. HAVE FAITH: *I see a lot of things from up here that you can't see from where you are. Have faith in Me that I know what I'm doing. Trust Me, you wouldn't want the view from My eyes. I will continue to care for you, watch over you, and meet your needs. You only have to trust Me. Although I have a much bigger task than you, it seems as if you have so much trouble just doing your simple part. How hard can trust be?*

7. SHARE: *You were taught to share when you were only two years old. When did you forget? That rule still applies. Share with those who are less fortunate than you. Share your joy with those who need encouragement. Share your laughter with those who haven't heard any in such a long time. Share your tears with those who have forgotten how to cry. Share your faith with those who have none.*

8. BE PATIENT: *I managed to fix it so in just one lifetime you could have so many diverse experiences. You grow from a child to an adult, have children, change jobs many times, learn many trades, travel to so many places, meet thousands of people, and experience so much.*

How can you be so impatient then when it takes Me a little longer than you expect to handle something on My to-do-list? Trust in My timing, for My timing is perfect. Just because I created the entire universe in only six days, everyone thinks I should always rush, rush, rush.

9. BE KIND: *Be kind to others, for I love them just as much as I love you. They may not dress like you, or talk like you, or live the same way you do, but I still love you all. Please try to get along, for My sake. I created each of you different in some way. It would be too boring if you were all identical. Please, know I love each of your differences.*

10. LOVE YOURSELF: *As much as I love you, how can you not love yourself? You were created by Me for one reason only—to be loved, and to love in return. I am a God of Love. Love Me. Love your neighbors. But also love yourself. It makes My heart ache when I see you so angry with yourself when things go wrong. You are very precious to me. Don't ever forget …*

After sitting, reading, and absorbing these mysteriously found guidelines, I had a moment of clarity: for longer than I was aware of, I had the fear of being without, of not having enough... and that's when a previous message from God resounded. When is enough, enough?

We cannot have fear and faith at the same time!

EVERYTHING HAS TO DO WITH NUMBERS

*O*n December 15, 2008, just two days after finding the "Ten Guidelines from God" in my dining room, I stood in the back of St. Veronica Church. Before I had pen in hand for my daily session with God, His voice startled me. "Everything has to do with Numbers. Deuteronomy."

I was totally surprised. I was barely set to write and these words came barreling out so suddenly. I mean I remembered Deuteronomy from Sunday school—it was a book in the Old Testament of the Bible—but I thought, *Gee, first God tells me everything has to do with math, and then He states the name of a book in the Bible!* I was perplexed!

The first thing I did was address what God had said about numbers. I took a piece of paper and wrote the letters of the alphabet in a line from left to right. Then I jotted the numbers in order under each letter, beginning with the number *one*, to designate a numerical identity for all the letters of the alphabet. I proceeded to spell the words *Jesus* and *numbers,* and wrote the corresponding digits on a piece of paper in order to play them in the upcoming lottery.

God must have been laughing Himself silly watching me do this crazy pairing to play the numbers in the lottery, which, I will embarrassingly tell you, I did do right after leaving church… and I will also tell you I did not win!

So, I went home, and the following night I had to look for something again in the dining room cupboard where the Ten Guidelines had appeared. I opened the cabinet door and in the exact same location where the three sheets of paper had dropped just days before sat a brand new boxed Bible a friend had given to me years before. This was too weird.

I set the box on the dining room table, took the top off, and with the Bible still in the box, I opened to a random page. When I fixed my eyes on the heading of that page, I read one word: Deuteronomy.

"This is something," I thought. Suddenly a few pages slipped from my fingers and what do you think I saw? A page entitled "Numbers"! The Book of Numbers came directly before the Book of Deuteronomy, a lesson forgotten from my Sunday school days, and a good reason for why I probably didn't win the lottery!

With my curiosity piqued now, I pulled out a chair and sat myself down, ready to read the Book of Numbers with the hope that I would understand what God meant by his words.

Everything has to do with Numbers.

Numbers are basically God's guidelines for His children on lifestyle, morals, and health. The book of Numbers is how God guided Moses to lead the people of Israel through the desert to the Promised Land in tribes that were numbered and counted. Because of the Israelite's disobedience and lack of faith, God forced them to wander through the desert for forty years as punishment.

The Book of Numbers refers to God's guidance, His journey with us toward Heaven. To move when He says to move, and to stay where we are when He instructs us to be still. To refuse to go back to an old place, a place of bondage or oppression, and to follow God into all the great things He has for us. Chapter after chapter expounds on the importance of faithfulness, holiness, and trust, and God's wrath against disobedient people, reminding us of the spiritual war we continuously face.

This made me think back to several of my church visits, when God told me to be still or to slow down. I can only guess how much I must have frustrated Him, because anyone who knows me knows I never sit still. I was always rushing and rushing and rushing, filling my days with activities and work, which helped me avoid looking at my own life.

God wants us to pause at times so that we might reflect and examine what is happening in our lives and evaluate whether we are living the way He wants us to live. With distractions, we cannot turn to God and hear His words of love and encouragement. Many of us create distractions to avoid a real assessment of ourselves and our personal environment. When we fail to reflect and correct, situations worsen, relationships begin to crumble, and suddenly we feel devastated and angry. The realization may be painful, but it is the resolution that will set us free.

In order to make time to reflect and examine our lives, we need to put down the electronic games, cell phones, turn off the television, stop complaining, and begin focusing on relationships, friends, community, culture, and universal peace. We need to learn to forgive by letting go of any judgment in order to free ourselves of negativity. Forgiveness doesn't mean what happened was right, it means you are willing to let it go.

We need to make time to create peace in our lives, time to talk to God and seek His help, because He wants to give us strength. He wants us to lean on Him and trust Him. He wants to heal our broken hearts and release us from sadness, bitterness, and fear. He wants us to be obedient, loving, considerate people because only then can we begin to love others. And all of us can pass that love forward and make it become universal.

INTERCESSOR

*A*s 2009 quickly approached, I paused to reflect on my life. I was saddened by past transgressions and I wanted to be forgiven. I began to pray for forgiveness when I heard the voice of Jesus, who in Christianity is God's son, say, "Don't worry, I will intercede for you."

That was like taking the express lane to Heaven! Jesus interceding on my behalf was giving me immediate attention from God.

I have come to realize that I, too, at times have become an intercessor, and many other people can be as well. I believe God's intent is for us to intercede for each other. For us to be an intercessor, it is important to revere God and His power and to desire giving up our time on behalf of another person who has challenges beyond their scope of understanding—which means forgetting about our own desires and needs, provided it does not conflict with our vocation and God's law.

We can allow God to interrupt our so-called busy lives if we practice unconditional love and have the confidence that He will hear us, remembering that we may be called upon to pray for people we may dislike, fear, or who may offend us. If there is to be any healing in our world, we must be willing to forgive and pray to our God for guidance in hopes of obtaining restoration of peace and order.

The following Catholic Christian prayer by the 13th Century St. Francis of Assisi sums it up perfectly:

Peace Prayer Of St. Francis

Lord, make me an instrument of your peace, Where there is hatred,
let me sow love; Where there is injury, pardon;

Where there is doubt, faith;

Where there is despair, hope;

Where there is darkness, light;

Where there is sadness, joy.

Grant that I may not so much seek to be consoled as to console;

To be understood as to understand;

To be loved as to love;

For it is in giving that we receive,

It is in pardoning that we are pardoned,

And it is in dying that we are born to eternal life.

Every time I read this beautiful prayer, it brings tears to my eyes. I believe it sums up exactly what an intercessor should be.

In closing this chapter, I'd like to share with you an interesting experience that is somewhat related to the topic of intercession through the teachings of the Catholic Church.

In Catholicism we are taught to honor the Blessed Virgin Mary, mother of Jesus, who always does the will of God. It is believed that she can intercede for mankind by presenting our petitions to her son, Jesus, who then presents them to His Father.

I had an experience that certainly would challenge any non-believer of the Blessed Virgin Mary's presence during prayer.

In December of 2008, as I made my way to the statue of Jesus in the back of St. Veronica Church, I noticed two women in a pew not far from me reciting the Rosary.

Kneeling in front of Jesus, I began to pray and became acutely aware of something unusual in the female voices behind me. I heard the two women I had previously observed recite each Hail Mary, but during every recitation of the Lord's Prayer a third female voice—distinctly different than the original two—would join in, and her voice would resonate through the air. Three or four times I turned around to see where the third woman was sitting, only to see the original two women in the pew.

I finally turned back, perplexed, looked up to Jesus and asked, "Who does the third voice belong to?" He responded, "That ... is my Mother." My jaw just about dropped.

HEALING MASS

Saint Veronica Church conducts a monthly service called a Healing Mass. In Catholicism, a healing mass is unique in that the entire focus is on using prayer for healing, whether it be the need to heal something physical, like a broken leg; spiritual, like getting closer to God; or emotional, like relationship problems.

When I attended these Masses, I either focused on something specific that I knew needed healing physically or emotionally, or I used the prayers as a way to rejuvenate my spirit in order to be more forgiving and enlightened.

The Healing Mass consists of worship, praise, and Holy Communion. Afterward the lights are dimmed to a soft glow, and soothing music is played. Those who wish to receive prayers for hands-on healing join in line down the center aisle of the church and wait their turn to be received by a prayer group.

Each prayer group consists of two to three people, one of whom stands behind the participant and acts as a catcher for those that may become weak and fall to the floor, known in the charismatic church as "resting in the spirit" or "being slain in the spirit." In some instances, the prayers for healing are performed while the participants are seated, which negates the need of the catcher.

Each participant, after being welcomed by a prayer group, states their first name and the type of healing they seek. A group member then anoints the participant's head with oil as the other members lay their hands on the receiver and begin to chant prayers, acting as intercessors to God.

On January 20, 2009, prior to the start of Healing Mass, I had an epiphany: I realized that when I brought my problems to God I was always trying to take them out of my body and hand them over to Him, instead of allowing His spirit to enter me and handle my problems from within. I pondered that throughout the Mass and while I waited my turn to be received by a prayer group. And, in that dim light, I felt so overwhelmed with God's love it was almost surreal.

When I was received by one of the prayer groups and asked if there was anything in particular I wanted to pray for, my response was to be filled with the Holy Spirit. My head was then anointed with blessed oil as the group began to chant individual prayers simultaneously. My body went limp as a catcher guided it to the floor. As I surrendered, I could feel the Holy Spirit fill me.

Lying on the floor along the base of the altar, I felt an amazing peace envelop me, as if I was on another plane and all the elements of the real world no longer existed. Feeling as if I was in a dream state, I began to recite in my mind the scripture, *Behold, I stand at the door and knock. If anyone hears My voice and opens the door, I will come unto him and dine with him and he with Me (Revelation 3:20).* I had committed this verse to memory from a prayer card Father Williams gave to me the day of my first healing, the first day of the rest of my life.

The warmth I first felt began to expand into white light which got brighter and brighter until it seemed as if there were headlights shining through my closed eyelids. Nothing seemed to exist but me and this magnificent bright light. For some reason unknown to me at the moment, my eyes followed down my right leg and I saw Jesus in a glowing white robe standing at my right foot. I heard myself repeat the words, *Behold, I stand at the door and knock. If anyone hears My voice and opens the door, I will come unto him and dine with him and he with Me (Revelation 3:20).*

I could feel the tears flow from the outer corners of my eyes as I said, "Lord please, please forgive me. For all this time I never realized that the door I was to open was to my soul, my being, my body, my spirit house, not the material house I live in. You have been knocking all these years and I never let You in!"

I never realized until that moment that I was to invite him into my body! My body is my house and my heart is my door where He knocks. All this time I was trying to take my sufferings out of my body and hand them to Him. Now as I invited Him into my body, I felt an energy moving and shifting, His love racing through me. I was acutely aware of sporadic bursts of a golden yellow light that permeated the bright white light that surrounded me.

As I bathed in the warmth of the light, the music from my 8th grade graduation ceremonies, "Walk Hand in Hand With Me," began to play in my mind, and I realized I had been humming that tune all week.

> *Walk hand in hand with me through all eternity,*
>
> *No greater love have we, walk hand in hand.*
>
> *Be not afraid for I am with you all the while,*
>
> *So hold your head up high and look up to the sky.*

As the music continued playing in my mind, I had a vision of Jesus dancing with me. Love and joy filled our hearts as we danced on a hillside blanketed with lush green grass and bright, colorful wildflowers.

I was so moved by the beauty of this scene, and when I paused and looked toward my right foot, Jesus lowered Himself toward me and extended His right hand toward mine. I proffered my right hand to him in acceptance of His invitation as He took it, gently and slowly pulling my spirit out of my physical body toward him. He smiled and said, "Come with Me."

I felt myself become lighter and lifting from the body that looked just like me lying on the floor. I rose up toward Jesus... releasing first from my head and shoulders, then my torso, thighs, and knees. I was able to separate my entire left side including my foot; but my right side would only release to my ankle.

And when I was to release the last part, my right foot, I pulled back! I wouldn't allow myself to let go any further... I was afraid. I began to feel squeezing pains across my entire chest, which made me think I was having a heart attack by letting go, and my fear was that I'd die and never come back.

After my spirit self got completely back into my physical self, the squeezing sensation in my chest subsided. I looked at Him and asked, "Will I die?"

He smiled and responded, "You'll never die, come with Me."

I explained that I knew my spirit would never die, but I questioned whether my earthly body would die of a heart attack and be left behind? I expressed I wasn't ready to leave the physical world permanently. I just felt I couldn't let myself go completely.

My head then slumped to the right toward my shoulder, and I felt two gentle hands envelope my lower face to ever so slowly and deliberately turn my head back upward toward the ceiling—or the sky. I realized, as with the lyrics to the song "Walk Hand in Hand with Me," the Lord wanted me to walk hand in hand with Him and to "look up to the sky."

I could feel tears running down my cheeks as He again extended his arm to invite me a second time to join Him. I did the same progression of separation until I was to release my right foot ... and, again, I felt the squeezing in my chest and resisted letting go completely. My spirit self then fully joined my physical self and the squeezing sensation in my chest again subsided.

We repeated this invitational process for a third time with the same outcome. I felt so badly that I'd allowed my humanness, my fear, to prevent me from trusting Him. I asked God to forgive my fears, that I truly regretted not going, for there was a Divine peace within that glorious warming light.

After what seemed to be a half hour, I slowly regained a consciousness back in my physical body, blinking my eyes open as if waking from a deep sleep. One of the prayer group members sensed my exhaustion and gave me a hand to sit up. I returned to a sense of here and now, and slowly stood so I could make my way to a chair and sit down. During the fifteen minutes I sat in this extremely relaxed state, I reflected on my experience and regretted my shortcomings that allowed fear to stand in the way of such an honor.

My thoughts gathered and my strength regained, I prepared to stand and leave when the woman who anointed me earlier approached. Without me telling her what I had experienced, she kissed and hugged me while she smiled, telling me I was going to be just fine. It was as if she was God's messenger and no explanation was necessary.

The following day I spoke to Father Williams. I was so moved about the happenings from the night before and had questions about my experience. He said I should not have been afraid, that I would have been fine and that I should go the next time the Lord invites me. Father Williams explained that only a special few ever receive that type of invitation and most likely the pressure I had felt in my chest was nothing but sheer anxiety caused by my fear of the unknown.

It is amazing what we can do to ourselves.

On the second day after this experience, January 24, 2009, I walked toward the back of the church, pen in hand, when I heard the Lord say, "Why were you afraid to come with Me? I would have shown you everlasting life."

I asked, "Would I have died?"

He answered, "No, I would have shown you for others. Don't be afraid. I love you. Thank you for coming to Me and making Me the most important person in your life."

TEN COMMITMENTS

I awoke on January 27, 2009, being told by God about these ten commitments we are to make to each other:

> *Grace* – *to commit to acts of kindness as we journey along together; being gracious to give, listen, and forgive in the same respect as we want to receive, be heard, and be forgiven.*

> *Healing* – *through grace we cannot only attempt to heal ourselves, but be instrumental in assisting others to heal mentally, physically, and/or spiritually.*

> *Humility* – *begin to be more humble and respectful to others, and put less importance on ourselves.*

Integrity *– be consistent with and have sound principles behind our actions, values, morals and honesty.*

Love *– show unconditional love to heal broken hearts, which can heal broken families, which can ultimately heal the world of bitterness, anger, and fear.*

Parenting *- be nurturing mothers and fathers who will unconditionally love, protect, support, and encourage the next generation so they will live these ten commitments.*

Purpose *– go forth with intention and determination each and every day, for without purpose, we are nothing.*

Sanctity *– make a commitment to deepen our religious faith and become more prayerful.*

Silence *– with inner stillness reflect and gain clarity for spiritual growth and transformation.*

> **Thankfulness** – *show more gratitude toward God for our redemption and restoration.*

On January 29, 2009, I received a divine message to be present for the noon Mass at St. Veronica's, which was odd because I normally didn't attend that mass. I was curious as to why I should be there, so I arrived early and sat in a pew in the right rear of the church to be silent and pray.

Although there was no music playing, I heard the hymn "I Heard the Voice of Jesus Say" repeat itself in my mind. The lyrics seemed to refer to my recent experiences with the Lord …

I Heard The Voice Of Jesus Say

I heard the voice of Jesus say,

"Come unto Me and rest;

Lay down, thou weary one, lay down

Thy head upon My breast."

I came to Jesus as I was,

Weary and worn and sad;

I found in Him a resting-place,

and He has made me glad.

I heard the voice of Jesus say,

"Behold, I freely give

The living water; thirsty one,

Stoop down and drink and live."

I came to Jesus, and I drank

of that life-giving stream.

My thirst was quenched, my soul revived, and now I live in Him.

I heard the voice of Jesus say,

"I am this dark world's Light.

Look unto Me; thy morn shall rise,

And all thy day be bright."

I looked to Jesus, and I found

In Him my Star, my Sun;

And in that Light of Life I'll walk

Till traveling days are done.

Horatius Bonar and John B. Dykes. "I Heard the Voice of Jesus Say"
(No. 277) in The Lutheran Hymnal.

The homily at this mass spoke to how we are broken, that we hunger and thirst for the Word of God and that our daily bread is for spiritual nourishment. I realized then how much we all needed to follow the ten commitments as spiritual nourishment in order to quench our hunger for peace and harmony within ourselves and our relationships. And that is the beginning to worldwide healing.

I also was able to relate spiritual nourishment with the commitment of *purpose* because when I awake each day with purpose, I become energized with action, which leads to a sense of accomplishment, which results in a sense of self-satisfaction. Therefore, leading my life with daily purpose, I became a better version of myself, which led to better relationships. I realized all of us have to start somewhere, and that somewhere is within ourselves.

That evening I had a dream …

> *There was a house with wooden floors—no furniture, no kitchen, just one big room, reminding me of a tree house. There were three or four children in their early to mid teens in the house who seemed to be lost.*
>
> *I spoke with them and offered for them to come stay with me and we could figure this out together. They were so glad that they danced in celebration.*

As they were dancing, I saw headlights followed by a small custom painted pickup truck pull up to the house. Out of the brand new, shiny vehicle stepped a man in work clothes, sporting a growth of fresh green grass on his lower face in place of stubble. We smiled at each other as he saw the children and joined in their dance, creating a feeling of peace and harmony.

When I awoke I realized that the children in the dream represented God's children, like you and me. In the beginning of the dream they were spiritually impoverished, without purpose; they hungered for meaning. I, as their intercessor, entered the dream to let them know they were not alone. Once they knew this, the children began to celebrate the good news and the room was illuminated with light from the truck.

I felt the headlights represented the light of God, and the truck and work clothes likened to that of His son, the carpenter, whom He sent to us to save us. We are lost (sinners) and Christ saves us (Redeemer).

The dance was a celebration of life, of thanks, joy, and sustenance, which explains why there was no need for food or furniture in the house.

Jesus coming to the door reminded me yet again of *Revelation 3:20, Behold, I stand at the door and knock; if anyone hears My voice and opens the door, I will come in to him and dine with him and he with Me.* He came to the door, we invited Him in, and there was dancing, healing, and celebration. He is our sustenance, our spiritual food, our daily bread. He provides all we need. We are His children, His family.

What a beautiful dream.

WHY ME LORD?

*O*n February 9, 2009, I was thinking of this book before I went to bed and I asked, "Why me Lord?"

His response was, "Because you hear Me and you want to please Me. Because you are not perfect, yet the beauty that surrounds you will make people want to listen to My Word. As a child, you waited for Me, and I have been preparing you for decades.

"With all sincerity and your attempts to perfect your honesty, you have made Me proud of you. I have watched you grow like a flower and bloom into a beautiful young woman, mature and gracefully aging because of your faith, love, and trust in Me. Be an example for others to follow; take down My words and share them with the world, for whatever I say to you, I say to the world.

"Janice, I want you to be My intercessor, to help the world find peace, to leave their egos at the door, to love and honor themselves and each other, to want to make the world better for their children.

"Through your quest to have this intimate relationship with Me, I am able to keep your attention on the task at hand. You are My spokesperson, messenger, purveyor of the Word of My Father, God. Tell one and tell all.

"Share these, My messages, till I cometh, for I shall come again.

"Selah."

The following day I so looked forward to returning to St. Veronica Church! When I saw Jesus, He said, "I am so happy to see you, Janice!

I responded, "I am so happy to see you too! How do I say thank you? "

"You say thank you to Me every day," He said. "You say thank you when you smile. You say thank you when you weep in joy. You say thank you when you come to me and pray. You say thank you when you make others happy. You say thank you when you help someone across the street. You say thank you when you are in awe of the moon, the sun, the flowers, the birds, all my creations. You say thank you when you come to church and drop on your knees to thank Me. You say thank you when you write My words and share them."

He later told me to "Spread the Good Word to all—everywhere, everyone, every language—now and forever. Go in Peace."

As I turned to leave, overwhelmed with not only love, but also a huge responsibility, I heard, "Blessed child print this book. It is for the world to see. Thank you. God is with you now and always. Selah."

We continued meeting every day. I was always so full of enthusiasm looking forward to my date with Jesus!

There were times when Jesus would smile humorously as my whirlwind self would be flying into church, skidding to a stop before Him. One day, with His sense of humor, He said, "Sit, take a load off your feet."

I smiled and lovingly inquired, "What do I do to deserve your love?"

"You come to Me and share with Me. You share your life with Me and I embrace it. And I embrace you! Show Father Williams what I have written. Please tell him it is of the utmost importance to be published here and worldwide to all faiths, to all colors, and to all ethnic backgrounds.

"Share one and share all the Word of the Lord, for I am one and the same. All you understand My word. No one should shun it. Be My messenger. Now and forever may peace be with you, My love. Come back with the print out and we will work on the book together."

It was such a nice meeting today. My Lord seemed more relaxed and happy than during prior visits. I cannot imagine what His days are like!

As Jesus had instructed, I made arrangements to meet with Father Williams in the rectory to discuss the dictations so far. He had been aware of some of them from previous conversations we had. During this visit, the priest asked me to read aloud various passages, which led to some very good discussions.

One discussion expounded on my experience from the Healing Mass in January when Jesus took me by the hand and asked me to go with Him. Father said that Jesus was calling me to go to show me the mysteries of the other side. He explained that the Torii Gate symbol I had been shown months ago was a precursor to the Healing Mass experience, preparing me to go through the gate and learn the mysteries.

Later I heard God's voice say, "Yes, I will come again for you and show you the riches of Heaven."

DIVINE INTERVENTION

*D*ivine intervention is a miracle caused by God's active involvement in the human world, and it was the guidance I was in need of when I was figuring out how to present this book.

I had all my notes from church and from hours of research; all of God's messages had been transcribed. I had helped friends and acquaintances when they were in need of spiritual guidance by emailing His daily word, and they were so inspired, they asked to receive copies of God's messages on a regular basis. I received many written testimonials stating how these daily dictations made a difference in their lives.

I had previously met with Father Williams to discuss the transcriptions, and I now had all the ingredients to begin this book… and then suddenly I got distracted, distracted by work, by activities, by life, but mostly by fear. Fear of the unknown, I suppose.

I thought about all of the people that could quote scripture, which I could not. I began to think I wasn't good enough to write His word, not smart enough, not well versed enough, not educated in Christianity enough. Who would think I would be a person God would choose to speak to? I wasn't a martyr or a saint, just an ordinary girl in ordinary times. Why on earth would He want me? I was worried about what nonbelievers would think, that they might say, "Who is she that claims to hear messages from God?"

My daily journey still continued and so did my weariness. On March 6, 2009, Jesus spoke as I readied myself for dictation. "You are tired, I am tired too. You must take refuge in Me, My child. Rest and rejuvenate. You do too much for too many. Now is your time and you must take it. Take rest and then start My book. Get it done. Be still thy heart, be patient. Together I will show you the way. I love you always. Amen." And in my tiredness, I wept and then heard, "Just trust … it is a very solemn time."

As per His instructions, I took about five days off to rest, but it felt like months. I missed our time together; I missed our love, friendship, and camaraderie. I felt as though I were suffering a loss.

And I was suffering a loss, a loss within myself. This rest period and my abstinence from my daily visits caused me to slip back into the same uncertainty I'd now been feeling for weeks, lacking the confidence to continue to work on this book.

Negative emotions began to creep in. I became critical of myself and others. Most importantly, I had lost my inner peace, the peace that kept me calm, centered, and focused on the task at hand, the peace that flowed into my daily life. I started to feel on edge, irritable, impatient, and more than anything I was in want of the Lord.

I realized that although I prayed regularly, there was no substitute for attendance. My daily visits left me feeling renewed and rejuvenated in His love, peace, and grace. I was so thankful for God, my best friend and the love of my life. He was always there to listen, guide me, and love me no matter what came my way.

Although I heard God tell me often of the importance of proceeding with this book, and that He would guide me, my problem was a lack of confidence. I feared that no one would believe that God would have someone like me create His book.

I prayed about my shortcomings and on March 25, 2009, God answered my prayers with His first intervention. I had a business meeting with a man I had never met before who began to speak with me about having faith in God. Our business meeting had nothing to do with religion, and yet the man insisted at the end of the meeting that I listen to a CD of a sermon from his church, he said for some reason he knew I needed to hear it.

I graciously accepted the CD knowing in my heart that God was at work. I listened to the sermon and understood the message. I needed to stay on fire for God and stay filled with the Holy Spirit. "Stay on fire for God. There's no limit where God will take you."

The sermon confirmed that God wants a relationship with us and is always speaking to our hearts. He wants to take us places we've never gone, give us things we've never had, and tell us things we never knew. I couldn't help but think back to the Healing Mass when Jesus wanted me to go with Him to learn of things never spoken and how I allowed my fear to hold me back from such an experience.

I was reminded that I was God's vessel and I needed to do as He asked of me.

The following day when I returned the CD to the man who had unknowingly become God's messenger, I thanked him for sharing the sermon with me.

As I turned to leave, my business contact said, "You need to leave your job. Work diligently and prudently to get someone else to handle your business so God can minister through you. You are very useful to Him."

I felt God confirming His Divine plan as He spoke to me through this business contact.

I went back to church to apologize to God, and before I could speak, He said, "I am so sad, so sorrily disappointed in you and all. Where is this going? Please, I ask you—move forward. Amen."

I asked God to forgive me. "I am sorry Lord, please forgive me. I am waiting for this and waiting for that ..."

With a sigh, He interrupted, "Just write. Write and write and write until they come." (I didn't know who "they" were at the time, but I now believe "they" were the writing coach, editor and graphic artist who were divinely placed in my path to finalize this book.)

I began to weep. "Oh Lord, bring me peace that I may keep my focus on you! I keep dwelling on the past and worrying about the future instead of living in the now."

He said, "Be still My child. I worry about you. Oh, My child, I hear your pain. It is hard. You are too filled with emotion. You don't understand what is going on. Your future will come in the future, its own time. Peace and healing. It is all for a purpose. Trust in Me, your Lord."

I so much wanted to hurry to find an agent or publisher to help me get the book prepared and printed. I felt alone. I was researching authors of spiritual books to see who their agents or publishers were for leads.

During all of my frustration, God presented another messenger as His second intervention, an alter boy from my parish, while I was sitting in a back pew taking my customary dictation. As the sun's rays softly illuminated the back section where I sat, I became aware of this young man strolling up and down the center aisle along the opposite end of my pew. At one point I looked up and our gazes met. And, as if an invitation, he walked sideways down the pew to me to ask what I was writing. I explained it was the Word of God and of my spiritual journey. The young man known as Tommy enthusiastically told me how much he, too, loved God, that he was an altar boy, as was his dad previously.

Tommy asked if I would read some passages from my journal while he waited for his parents to arrive. There was something awesome about a young person asking to hear the word of God and to experience their deep desire to want a better relationship with Him. After I read several passages it was clear that he was very much in tune with the Lord as he told me how the messages had personal meaning for him. He asked when I would be back so he could listen to more of the messages from God.

After seeing Tommy several more times when I was writing in church, I realized that God brought Tommy to me to demonstrate that His messages were for everyone, not just people of different faiths, but people of all ages as well.

The third Divine Intervention came months later in a rather unusual way. I was home planning to get some things accomplished and get to bed early when I clearly heard God's message for me to go to a local pub where I occasionally ate or met friends. I had already changed and I really didn't want to go out and face the cold air again, but the voice was adamant, so I got dressed again and off I went.

I had no idea why I was going, but I had learned from past experiences that when I hear God speak I must heed. I don't frequent bars alone, so I had made up my mind that if there was no one there I knew, I was going to leave and go home.

I drove only ten minutes to reach my destination, and as soon as I walked in the door a bartender I knew was standing right in front of me! The place was really busy, and he saw I was awkwardly alone, and suggested I sit at the bar with a gentleman whom he called Bill. So I sat down, introduced myself, and told him that the bartender suggested I sit next to him. He seemed a bit standoffish at first, so I began chatting, believing that perhaps this chance connection was part of my mission, for I knew all the events and meetings I was instructed to attend previously were for a reason, and it was my job to follow directions. I trusted that my purpose would eventually unfold.

My conversation with Bill eventually led to church and prophesy. I told Bill about the messages I had been receiving at St. Veronica Church, and he asked if Jesus had given me a date for the end of the world. What? A date for the end of the world? Bill went on to explain that some people believed the world would end on May 21 in the year 2011. I explained that I had never heard of that, but was willing to research it.

We talked for a bit more, and before parting our ways, we exchanged email addresses so I could send some of God's messages to Bill as he had requested.

The next morning, I awoke to the following message from Bill, or should I say from God through Bill:

> *Thank you for a well-spent time,*
>
> *"Seeing" is believing, and so sublime.*
>
> *Your wit, charm, outlook, so, so bold,*
>
> *well conversant to behold.*
>
> *Pursue your calling, helping others,*
>
> *negate the naysayers with their druthers.*
>
> *Check out the future sent from heaven,*
>
> *with emphasis on the 2011.*

If time is short, make the most;

bring the flock towards the "Host."

He'll guide you further, this you know,

Show no fear, with "Him" you'll grow.

Take your time and do what's best,

you'll earn your place for the final rest.

AMEN..................BC

And so, I went back to writing my, oops, His book :)

I was figuring out how to present this book. Do I use daily dates? Do I separate His messages from the story? Should I consider using pictures? I prayed for guidance again that Sunday morning and received an answer within moments: go to five o'clock mass.

And, as always, Divine Intervention struck again as I listened to Father Chuck's Homily at 5 p.m. that day. He explained that when we are told we have a calling, and we ask, "Why me?" the answer is "Why not?" We need to step outside our comfort zone to the other side of fear, and just do it without worry of what others may think.

When the Mass ended, I went to the back of the church and thanked Jesus for His message. I told Him that I realized how important it is to marry someone of your own faith who will share and practice it with you.

Then I thought I heard Him ask me to marry Him! I remember my face crinkled up as if I must have misunderstood. I said, "What?" I heard again, "Will you be my bride?"

I didn't understand; I was flabbergasted. Marry the Lord? Could I have misunderstood? Why would He ask me? And how in the world could I marry Jesus? I heard Him say I was to wear a wedding band on my right hand in remembrance.

So I went home and got my deceased grandmother's sliver of an etched gold band and slipped it on my right ring finger. To my amazement, it fit me perfectly. I was still bewildered as to why I was even doing this and, as it had happened so many times before, I investigated in order to understand.

I had never heard of a Bride for Jesus, nor anything even close to it, so with the ring on I went to my computer and researched the term and, boy, was I surprised!

Matthew 9:15 refers to Jesus as the bridegroom whom has been taken away from us. We are told that He will come again and descend from heaven to bring His bride (us) away with Him to His Father's house.

Matthew 24:36 states that no one knows about the day or the hour, not even the angels in heaven, nor Jesus, only God. And Matthew 25:6 states that at midnight the cry rang out "Here's the bridegroom! Come out to meet him!"

Throughout the Bible, all the way through to the Book of Revelation, there is mention of the wedding, and we, as the bride, need to be prepared. Throughout my transcriptions God has been saying, *"the time is now."*

In Conclusion

*W*e must unite and find peace within ourselves, our families, work places, communities, governments, and countries.

We must universally know and understand that there is one and only one God, the one God we all worship. Perhaps we belong to different churches or speak different languages. It does not matter; there is one true God who loves us all.

I was thinking of this as I nestled myself beneath some trees to shade myself from the strong sun and became keenly aware of the foliage above me. Several large woodland trees had branches overlapping each, together providing shade and protection. However, if I looked closely, most leaves were imperfect, either eaten, marred by insects or disease, ravaged by weather, or simply deformed. Then I looked at a section of woodland further away, and all these trees appeared to be perfect.

Only then did the revelation come to me. God created the woodlands like families, and the trees, family members.

None of us individually are perfect. We are all flawed in some way or another. Yet, as a group, we have strength, endurance, and protection.

Our parents weren't perfect; however, they tried to provide the best shade and protection they were capable of. The stronger their roots, the more they were able to provide a secure environment for us. The weaker roots and holey leaves provided less shade and protection.

I also realized that it didn't matter if the woods were made up of many varieties of oaks, maples, and ash. Eventually they all grew together and joined together for one greater purpose.

What a wonderful example they have provided for ages and no one understood the message. We all come in varieties, colors, textures, and have unique differences, but if everyone on this planet stood together, we would become less imperfect. We could join in harmony to protect, shelter, and provide for our earth and its beings.

CLOSING

Thank you Jesus for not only being my best friend, but for never leaving my side, even when I didn't want to be with myself; for loving me and tending to me, encouraging me, thanking me, teaching me life lessons, and embracing me when I thought no one was there. You are the love of my life!

And thank you Mary, Mother of God, for bringing your Beloved Son into this world, for enduring the inequities of others with your head high and being such an integral part of our lives.

And Joseph, to whom so many forget, I thank you, too, for your insights, your protection, and your patience.

I love you all.

Thanks be to God Almighty, now and forever.

Selah.

Hush, My child... you are My light to the world. I need you to spread My Word among My people. It is never too late. It is almost too late

I belong to all faiths, all colors, and all ethnic backgrounds. Share one and share all the word of the Lord, for I am one and the same. All you understand My word. No one should shun it. Be My messenger. Now and forever may peace be with you.

Verily I say unto you of all faiths, you had better take heed, take warning to My words. For if you cannot make peace now, you will all be very, very sorry. This is only the beginning.

Raise your hearts. Raise them up to Me, your Lord. For I am the God of everyone.

>   *I am your God,*
>   *and your God,*
>   *and your God,*
>   *and your God.*

The Supreme God. The Supreme Being of all.

My messages are of an urgent matter and you cannot waste anymore time. People of the world unite with one another and stop domestic violence, stop regional violence and the world will stop its' shame and corruption which is destroying all I have created.

My deepest of disappointments is the lack of respect and love. Your spirit must rise above all else.

This is a serious matter. I am not bargaining with anyone. You must yield to My word.

The world is filled with treachery, violence and anger. Go forth into the world and love.

World fighting must stop! Enough is enough! This is all about ego now. I say if you are really a man of religion you will put down your guns and walk away.

Be at peace with your families.
Be at peace with your brethren.
Be at peace with your neighboring countries.

For how can you all claim to be men of God when you know I want you to fight not? For what I want, if you say I am your God, is to cease all fire, destroy all weapons of mass destruction, put down your guns, put down your guard, and open your hearts. Open them up to Me your God. Open them up to each other.

Make peace, leave your ego at the door.
Hold hands, celebrate life and the living,
your children, your mothers and fathers ...
those living and those that have gone
before you, for we shall all meet again.

Selah...

As to the world:
I am so sad, so sorrily disappointed in
My people. Where is this going? Please, I
ask you – move forward.

Amen

Be still thy heart:
Through patience and understanding
you will find peace and happiness.
Stop dwelling on the past, on the
times, on the bad news.
The Good News is here!
Here, right here in front of you!
Will you not open your eyes and see
it? Your ears and hear it? Hear My
voice through My words, the words
of the Lord...your Lord.

It is he who loves Me and trusts Me
that is willing to drop on his knees
and weep and thank Me for all of
My blessings bestowed on him.

He will find the Glory of God the
Father and the Kingdom of Heaven.
His will be the riches for eternity.

As to Bad Decisions:

Be silent in your thoughts.
This too shall pass. Take a break.

You cannot run away. It is time you
face your fears. Slay your own dragons.

You must maintain peace and love in your heart at all times. If you don't let those that make you angry in, then you don't have to work on getting them out.

Allow Me the privilege of assisting you in all you do. Give it all up to Me, your Lord, your God. For it is that which pleases Me most. Allow Me to share with you your joys and your sorrows ... your fears and hopes, all that you love and adore, as well as all vexations of your spirit.

For then we can all work together for the betterment and enlightenment of the world, and hopefully help heal it and ourselves.

Go in peace ...

I am God Almighty. You must respect Me always.
I sit on a throne among all the angels for all time.
I am the Judge, the Judge of the
quick and the dead; the loving Father of all
times, the punishing Father to those who
grossly offend Me.

I am in everyone. You should treat everyone like you would treat Me.

I forgive all who come to Me in honesty, bearing their hearts and souls.

Especially in today's unrest, we must generate and pass the love, peace and healing. You be the first. Pass it on. Play it forward.

The Lord giveth and the Lord taketh away. Be silent in your complaints. Be righteous in your thoughts. Be kind to each other. Share with each other. Prove to Me, your God, that you are indeed appreciative of My gifts to you and be willing to share them with others. Now is the time to rejoice in Me, not in your material things. For I am everlasting life.

Praise be to God.

It is blasphemy to use My name in vain.
Seal your lips from uttering My name unless
it is with praise and thanks.

Hold your tongue lest you should offend Me.

It is all too often and all too unaware of the
blasphemies uttered in your society.

© j.i. willett 2013

Lift your arms.
Lift them up to Me, your God.
Lift them up high and rejoice in
eternal life ...

You are the apple of My eye, a flower in the desert,
fresh rain on a glorious summer's day.

You are the light, the way for others to see a clearer path to
salvation. I will bless you always ... now and forever with
joy, abundance, health, wealth and love.

I embrace you always.

Be at Peace.
Go in Peace.
Flow in Peace.

Do not glorify yourself. It displeases Me. For how can you think you are more important than Me? How can you think your deeds are more important than Mine? For your deeds should be only to glorify Me, My name, and My name only.

For in glorifying Me, you have shown your love and dedication to Me. Through your deeds you are almsgiving to Me. Being good to one another is thanking Me for all I have given to you.

When you are in the midst of one who is glorifying himself, remain silent. Know that it is Me, your Lord, who is to get the praise. For the glory belongs to Me and to Me only.

Go in Peace
        Go in Love
                Go in Sanctity ...

With eyes wide open ....
giving thanks to Me, your Lord,
now and forever more.

As to your Children:
Let your love shine like there is no tomorrow. Let there be peace and understanding. May you always smile in the rain and laugh when it is cloudy.

May your children witness your joy, yet share in your sorrow. For it is in that sharing with them that breeds understanding and acceptance of all things, lest they be afraid.

Let them grow like a wildflower, experience all phases of life free and uninhibited, partially tamed, yet not stifling their individuality. Do not impose yourself on them, for how can a flower grow in a desert?

They are not you, they are themselves. You need only to be their nurturer, waterer, tender of the frail until such time as they can provide sustenance on their own. Then you must allow them that freedom, that opportunity of personal tending in order that they shall bear their own fruits in the sunshine of My love.

As to Money:

It has its' value, but the value can only be for providing for oneself and family. Do not put it above all else, for I am all else; I am your everything. I create the value within you. For when a man seeks Me, yet is counting his money, how can he hear My voice among the clanking of change? Shall he pay for his sins with money? No! He cannot buy his way out. Enjoy Me first, My love and blessings, and through those blessings you will be plentiful. I will provide a place for you to rest. I will provide for you a place for your weary head. Trust Me first and foremost and I shall provide you with riches beyond your belief. For there then will be plenty of money for your sustenance now, here on earth, and you will gain your riches in Heaven. Learn and understand the difference between earthly wealth and spiritual wealth. It is a wealthy man who kneels before Me, their Lord.

As to pain:

Do you not realize that most of your pain is self-inflicted? And yet you damn Me! For if you let Me guide you and take charge of your matters, there would be less drama. You create your own conflicts and dramas, and seek pain like a badge to prove to yourself and to others how traumatic the experience was. How silly you are. Do you not think that I, your Lord, don't know the difference? Could you not have waited for Me to handle those issues for you... to answer your prayers, your thoughts, your short comings? Could you not wait in silence and know I would be there for you?

And then... then you call My name when you are so far down to pull you up. And even then you fail to even hold your arm up for the rescue. How lazy can you be? I say to you, one and all, learn from these lessons. Read them over and over until you begin to understand. I realize you are only human and I do not expect you to be perfect, but I do expect that you try. Please, I ask of you, please come to Me and trust in Me and allow yourselves to please Me by asking for My help... and then wait for it.

As to Love:
Let it flow like the
rivers of time into your heart.

Assume nothing:

Do you really think you are in control? Do you really think you can second guess Me, your Lord? Why, when a man hears My voice and assumes not, who is he to say I am there for him? Ye that cometh in My house to pray and it is all selfishness, do you not know that you are a vexation to My spirit when you do that? When you come to Me not in honesty and worthiness? Assume nothing. For I, your Lord, am the only One who knows the outcomes of all your thoughts and prayers.

Hush... in silence you shall hear the answers. For they are always there for you. You just fail to listen, to see, to act upon My ways because they are not the outcomes you wanted. There then, so be it! I am growing weary in all My efforts to entertain you. These are My last words to you... go in peace, find peace, be at peace, world peace.Grow together, heal together, and remember Me your Lord for ever and ever. Praise be to God.

As to anxiety:
It's for the birds!!! Where did it come from? Who thought of
it? I never once told you to be anxious about anything, and
yet you all are filled with anxiety. Pills, stress relievers,
whatever... there is no stress relief such as in Me!

Lift up your hearts, lift them up high. Take deep breaths and
know, I say know, that there is nothing to be anxious about.
Be at peace. Be calm. Be thoughtful. Give praise. Be kind to
each other as I have previously asked of you.

As to worry:

Worry about nothing for I am your source of strength. When the winds blow and prevail for days, I will be your rudder and your sails. Have faith in Me now and forever more. Why worry yourself and take precious time from your life when you have no control over it? It is I who has control! It is I who knows what is best for you. It is I who will take care that you receive the proper outcome.

Therefore I say to you be patient in all you do and in all you see and in all you feel for it is only I who foresees the outcome. Relax from worry. Relax from fear. I know what is best for you and I will handle it.

Go in peace, be safe, be assured. Nothing can come from anxiety but weakness and sickness. Be not afraid for I am with you all the while. I am walking beside you. I am with you ALWAYS... ...

As to Purpose:

Go always in peace. Dwell in peace. Peace is silence. In silence pray. In prayer hunger for knowledge and understanding in all things. Ask for wisdom and for purpose. For without purpose you are nothing. Awaken each day with purpose. If you do not know what to do, then ask Me and allow Me to guide you to your destination. It is purpose that creates esteem. It is esteem that creates confidence, and in the confidence you will find peace. For with peace there can be no anger, no animosity… only peace.

As to Anger: leave it on the doorstep and your ego at the door. Do not enter in a house unless you can enter it in peace and love. Entertain not those individuals who are vexations to the Spirit. Only show love and leave in peace.

*How much do I love you?
I show you every day
through all those
you meet.*

As to Hate:
The world is full of hate. In homes, in families, in so-called friendships – the world is full of falsity. It is better to say 'I hate you', than to feign affection. Be at peace in your heart. Only then can you be cleansed of hate born of anger. Hate breeds violence.

Violence in the world and even in our own bodies… the re-enactment of anger will kill you. It harms us in so many ways. It breeds contempt. Contempt breeds violence, violence is where the world is today. Violent minds from violent hearts creating violent countries. Is there no other expression of oppression except through violence? I ask you this… If a man steps under your tree and steals an apple, will you kill him? Or will you take the time to learn of his inequities and be willing to share your fruits with him? Then is it that he is stealing, or is it that you have given through worldly compassion? Can a man not feel entitled to share of another man's fruits if there is an abundance, lest the unused portion go to waste?

As to provisions for you and others:
If mankind will honor Me and give thanks, I shall provide
for him and his family. It saddens Me not for those that
are defiled with money. It saddens Me most when others
suffer for the cruel acts of the selfish.

The selfish know full well who they are and have time to
repent and make good to their fellow man. Then they
shall be in My good graces again. But until such time, they
shall be Persecuted for they have greatly
disappointed Me. They have taken
My goodness and blessings and
defiled them. Shame be to those
whose names they know.
They know who they are
and must repent.

© j.i. willett 2013

As to Being Humble:

Not only should you humble yourself before Me, but you should humble yourself to your brethren. For it is they, too, that you have offended. Seek them out and ask for forgiveness. Settle your affairs with all whom you have met. Ask for mercy and blessings which shall follow you all the days of your lives, and then you shall be free.

Wait not until you are humbled in your frailty of age or debilitation. Become humble by choice. And in your humility do service for others. For this too shall please Me.

As to Pride:

The more proud you are,
the harder you will fall.
Therefore, it is easier to
voluntarily drop to your
knees.

As to Humility:

By all means be yourself. Do not be shameful nor commit shameful deeds. Be humble in all you do for I am your Lord, the way and the light. Humility is what brings you closer to Me. It is the foundation of your being. It is the basis for all mankind.

For to know humility brings you closer to Me. Practice humility in all you do. Patience and humility are the corner stones to true religion. For until one can experience humility, he is nothing. Until he can express humility, he is far from the truth.

For it is he who comes on his knees and begs for forgiveness that will be blessed and honored with goodness and mercy.

As to Abundance:
You will always have more than you think. You may deny it,
you may not believe Me, but if you open your eyes you will see
the truth and only the truth. Keep your eyes wide open through
the progressions of the day. If you can claim that you do not see
personal riches in My miracles then you are not seeing clearly.

Then you must take the blinders off your eyes lest you not see
where you are going and trip and fall. Lest you not see your
money or earthly riches which are all you think you own.

Do you not know that you own the air and the moon and the
sky? The flowers, the grass and the wonders of all nature? And
do you not know that I bless you with the ability to have more
if you so choose by giving you a body and mind capable of
doing more to earn more if money is what you seek?

But I tell you the abundance lies in My miracles. And My riches
will keep you, clothe you, feed you and protect you all the days
of your life.

As to Life's Journeys:
Journeys are good, especially of the heart. Smile and embrace each moment, good or bad, for each has value to the total equation.

Enjoy your journeys, for they are like flowers ... they unfold, bloom and are perennial.

As to obsession:
It is the root of all evil…money, things, people, arrangements.
When are you going to stop? You cannot compare yourself with
others, for I have made each of you special. For every time you
obsess, you have taken your focus off Me, your Savior. Obsess
over this and obsess over that. When is enough enough?

I say to you when a man has enough in his yard, why does he
look to his neighbor's yard to have validation? Why does he see
that there might be more and then obsess over it? Then he is
never happy with what I have provided him with because he
believes his neighbor has more. He becomes to feel cheated,
robbed of material things… never realizing all gifts are not
necessarily in the form of things. My gifts to each of you cannot
be measured one by one. For each of you are different and have
different gifts, talents, requirements. Therefore only I know when
and what you need. How dare you offend Me and complain and
obsess that what I have given to you is not good enough or is not
enough? Shame should be hanging o'er your head lest you wake
up and open your eyes and see what I have given to you and be
thankful. Be thankful unto Me, your Lord. For without Me you
would be nothing.

As to Balance:
What does balance have to do with anything?
It has to do with everything!
Without balance you cannot function properly.
You must divide your time into pods (segments).

©j.i. willett 2013

As to letting go:
When you are willing to give it up,
You will get it all back ... ...

Everything has to do with the Book of Numbers:
Move when I say to move, and stay when I instruct you
to be still.

Refuse any inclination to go back to an old place, a
place of bondage or oppression, and instead follow Me
into all the great things I have in store for you.

You cannot compare yourself to others.
You are a candle in your own light.
Shine your own beauty and embrace it.
Be proud of it. For
I am the truth, the way and the light.
Be bright. Be joyous. Be happy.
Rejoice in Me.

© j.i. willett 2013

*It is My wish to have all people come to Me
with their trials and tribulations.
Seek Me in all things ... in sorrow, in weakness,
in sickness, in health, in joy and prosperity.
Seek Me in those and I will be of assistance.*

Praise be to God on the Highest.

Come to Me often for I love that.
Stay strong, stay focused.
Do not be critical of anyone
or anything ... It doesn't matter.

Love with all your heart, like there is no tomorrow, like you never have before and may never have the opportunity to again ...

With passion and dedication,
With honesty and pleasure.

For this pleases me to no end.

I show you love every day
through others ...

© j.i. willett 2013

Be grateful for others
and rejoice in their
accomplishments and
happiness.

For it is in this state
that you will find peace
and learn your lessons
in life.

Bring all your sorrows and problems to Me and please Me.
I shall delight in that and take care to have you not suffer
consequences of the flesh or sin, for I am the way, the light
and forgiveness forever.

Trust in Me, for I am the only way to inner peace and
eternal light.

Go in peace.
Go with love in your heart.
Go with joy in your soul.

Bow your head in grace. Grace is what most lack. A lack thereof is an emptiness you will never be aware of until you have found it.

Grace reveals the beauty within you, within us all ... the depths of our understanding in all things. And whether you understand all things now or not, if you practice grace, it will help humble you.

For I love you with all My heart. I want only for your happiness and prosperity and acts of kindness to each other in all mankind. For what is a man without hands that can touch the earth or sky? Through My love I want for you to be complete.

Bow your heads first to Me. Then through grace, bow them to each other...

When those persons forsake you, love them. Be kind to them. They are not the enemy; the enemy harbors within us all and it is that enemy we must slay. It is the poison in our own hearts that must be purified. Through pureness we can see no evil, no hatred or anger. Purify yourself first and foremost, lest you judge someone else.

Where is the happiness?

You are all focused on the bad and fail to thank Me for My grace through all these times ... good and bad. When there is good, you forget Me. When there is bad, you forget Me. I am your Lord, your Savior. Please, please come to Me. Give thanks and praise for I am providing for you. In one way or another, I am. When one door closes, I open another. It may not be what you expected; however, I did hear you and have provided. Have you not yet seen that sometimes I provide for you through others? You are all a part of Me ... Me your Lord. Don't forsake Me. Verily, I look down upon you and wonder ... wonder where this is all going. For no one seems to hear My voice. Rise up. Lift your heads and hearts. Lift them up to Me, your Lord.

You are all My children.
You are a child of the
universe, no greater or
smaller than any other.
Remember this always, for
this is how peace will come
to the world. Only through
love and understanding...
the realization that you are
all My children and I love
you all the same. Respect
each other's differences as
much as you embrace your
likenesses. Offer yourself to
them. Be at peace with
them. Let them know
forgiveness is only as near
as the asking.

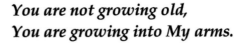

You are not growing old,
You are growing into My arms.

Don't move too quickly ... slowly and deliberately.
Think your thoughts before you speak. Analyze nothing.
Do everything. Listen to Me, delight in Me. Nothing
else exists – nothing, that is, that is permanent.

As the tides ebb and flow, so shall be the affections of
others, but My love will be steady and forthright
through heavy seas and storms; rain and clouds;
sun and moon ...

Everlasting
Ever fast
Ever long.
Forever ...

*Take the splinter out of your own eye
lest you be critical of others...*

Love is not just about ourselves. It goes much further than that. You all know it. Why do you not practice it? Why is everything centered around you? What makes you more special than your neighbor? Love your neighbor as you do yourself. Open your doors and invite them in. Invite all in. Why, you have yet to invite Me in. For how can you become a better person if you do not invite Me into your "house", your body, your soul? For I am to dwell with you, do you know that?

Open your doors, your hearts, to Me, your Lord, as well as your neighbors, your brethren, for that is where love and true happiness lie. Smile. Be at Peace. Be happy. Be Joyous. Be in Me and I in you.

© j.i. willett 2013

Be still thy heart. You are all suffering pain and anguish with the times at hand. You must remember My name and rest in it, in peace and understanding. Understanding that I, your Lord, will comfort you whilst none other can.

I, your Lord, will be strong when you are weak, bright when you are dull, steadfast when you lose your footing. Trust in Me, your Lord, and God. For all your needs will be fulfilled. Cry not except to cry unto me in thanksgiving and salvation; for I am your Lord and I shall come again in time. Raise up your heads. Raise them up to Me, your God. Rejoice with all your hearts and be glad for a new day cometh.

Hate not your enemies, but find the source of your anger. For it is that anger that is festering inside you that must be subdued.

Like the candles in the church, the eternal burning flames, so shall anger continue until you make the concerted efforts to extinguish it from your soul and this earth.

Lift your hearts, lift them up to Me. Rejoice in the freedom of peace and harmony.

Release the damaging thoughts, the hatred and fire, reduce yourself to love... for it is that which I admire. Peace be with you always...

Be pure in your thoughts for I know all you think.
Be pure in your deeds, for I see all you do.
I am the way and the light, now and forever more.

Be easy on yourself, take rest in My arms. Lie with Me, beside Me, beside the still waters of your soul. Restore yourself with Me, dwell with Me, trust in Me, love with Me. Divine mercy has forgiven you. Remember to tell others of My proclamations, dedications and promises to always be in their hearts... the Light and the Way now and forever more...

Everlasting,
Ever loving,
Ever encompassing.

Be not proud nor pompous in the things you do,
for that displeases Me. Come to Me with
thanksgiving and praise always.

Bow down your heads, bow them down to Me,
your Lord. Give praises to heaven and ask for
forgiveness. It is never too late to repent for all
your inequities.

As I give to you to please you, so shall you give
yourself to Me.

Be at peace with yourself.
Be at peace with your neighbors.
Be at peace with all mankind.

For negativity cannot exist where there is love. Negativity cannot exist where there is compassion and yearning for the truth... yearning to see the light and follow it. To give your sins up to the Cross and bear your sorrows in Me.

Like a flame flickers in the church, so shall it flicker in
your heart until it radiates goodness and mercy. Then
use that flame, that light, to show the way to those who
are lost.
Be a candle, be a light, be a beacon for Me ... and My love
will pave the way for others.
Spread the Good word to all
Everywhere
Everyone
Every language
Now and forever.

Trust in Me, your Lord, for I will provide.
I have never let you down.
I have come in the right time and the right place.
Not according to your plan, but to Mine.

Go in peace
Go in love
Go in sanctity ...

With eyes wide open ... and give thanks
To Me, your Lord.

When is enough enough?
It's time!

© j.i. willett 2013

For what more do you want Me to do? What more do you expect of Me? Do you not have any expectations of yourselves? Are you not responsible for anything? Should you not take responsibility for any of your actions or of the actions of the world? For I stand before you and weep... no, cry... for all the regrets you have. Regrets of this and regrets of that!

Enough is enough!
No blasphemy
No tantrums
No whining
No more –
Now is the time.

Now is the time to pull your bootstraps up and conquer the world. Your world. Your thoughts, your actions, your reactions and your heart. Your attitudes, which I might add, I am disappointed in many.

When you conquer yourself, so shall you and your brethren conquer the world.

Come unto Me. It is a dark moment. Lift up your heads.
Lift them up to Me. Lift up your hearts. Lift them up to Me,
your Lord. Hold them up high for I cometh and how can you
see Me   if you are looking down? Look up unto Me,
your   Lord , now and forever. Peace shall come
over   all the world . Wait and see. Mark My
words   for I know when and how . It shall not be
long My friends. Your time is running out. Make amends,
make peace, make restitution, solve your inequities for I am
at hand. Doubt Me not for I tell you the truth and only the
truth for it is Me, your Lord and God, who can save you. Yet
you can save yourself and you choose not to. Why? I ask
you. I have given you all the tools necessary and you still
complain and remain stuck. Stuck to the earth, material
matters, rights and wrongs, egos. Now is the time. Raise
your hearts up to Me, your Lord. Go in peace, make peace.
Make peace with yourself and your neighbors. Yourself and
your friends. Yourself and your families. Yourself and the
world. Now is the time. Trust in Me and My word.
Now and forever .

Be prepared,

the worst is yet to come ...

© j.j. willett 2013

Now is the time, today is the day.
Respect and honor Me, your Lord
and Father. For as the world comes
closer to the end as we now know
it, you will give thanks and praise.

It is Me who shall save you, Me
that shall rescue you, Me that will
protect your foot lest you strike it
on a rock. Therefore, trust in Me,
respect Me, praise Me and love
Me always ... love and respect Me
for all the days of your life.

Live each moment for itself...
and not dwell on the past nor look to
the future. For this moment is the
moment, and you shall never get it back.
It was a gift to you and it displeases Me
to know that this very moment may
have been given to you in vain.
Peace be to God.
Peace be to you all.
Amen
Selah

It is a grave situation here and everywhere... you wait and see. Find your hearts. Find them now. Look deep inside for the peace and joy within.

Verily I say unto you, this will be your well to draw from. When you think there is no place to go, go within. Remember your well, for I am there. I always have been. You have been distracted by external forces and thereby never knew it existed.

Be strong ... Be faithful ... Be Mine.
Always and forever ...
Amen,
God

Behold, I am the living water. I am the life, I am your daily bread. It is I of whom all things come. Behold, you must seek the Lord in all you do, in all you say, in all you think. It is I, the Lord, who is your constant provider.

Now and Forever may there be peace. For it is written that I am sustenance for all, the King and Ruler of all the heavens and the earth. As it was in the beginning, is now and ever shall be... world without end... Amen